ACT NOW

You are the hero of your own story, so don't let the biggest obstacle to achieving all your professional and personal goals be you. Remember, the world is a better place when you are better in it.

If you are ready to rewire the mindset to unstick and unlock your fullest potential, send an email to me at caryn_ross@spectabridgesolutions.com for a mindset business coaching session. Always believe in you!

The Key to Being a Highly Successful Woman

Self-Love: The Key to Lead, Empower, and Transform

Caryn Ross

THiNKaha®

An Actionable Success Journal

E-mail: info@thinkaha.com
20660 Stevens Creek Blvd., Suite 210
Cupertino, CA 95014

Published by THiNKaha®
20660 Stevens Creek Blvd., Suite 210, Cupertino, CA 95014
http://thinkaha.com
E-mail: info@thinkaha.com

First Printing: April 2019
Hardcover ISBN: 978-1-61699-320-7   1-61699-320-0
Paperback ISBN: 978-1-61699-319-1   1-61699-319-7
eBook ISBN: 978-1-61699-318-4   1-61699-318-9
Place of Publication: Silicon Valley, California, USA
Paperback Library of Congress Number: 2019902081

Trademarks

Warning and Disclaimer

Dedication

To my father, who taught me that anything is achievable if you have passion and purpose and work hard doing it.

To Ian, Eric, and Lisa: Dream big and never limit all the possibilities that await you.

Scott, thank you for always believing in me.

To all my girlfriends, who inspired me and were my role models as strong women who never limited their personal and professional successes. Never stop believing what you can achieve.

Publisher's Note

My wife read this book and loved it.

I also loved it.

So, men, although this book says it is for highly successful women, I highly encourage you to read it as well.

There's a lot to learn from this author.

How to Read a THiNKaha® Book

A Note from the Publisher

The AHAthat/THiNKaha series is the CliffsNotes of the 21st century. These books are contextual in nature. Although the actual words won't change, their meaning will every time you read one as your context will change. Be ready, you will experience your own AHA moments as you read the AHA messages™ in this book. They are designed to be stand-alone actionable messages that will help you think about a project you're working on, an event, a sales deal, a personal issue, etc. differently. As you read this book, please think about the following:

1. It should only take 15–20 minutes to read this book the first time out. When you're reading, write in the underlined area one to three action items that resonate with you.

2. Mark your calendar to re-read this book again in 30 days.

3. Repeat step #1 and mark one to three more AHA messages that resonate. They will most likely be different than the first time. BTW: this is also a great time to reflect on the AHA messages that resonated with you during your last reading.

After reading a THiNKaha book, marking your AHA messages, re-reading it, and marking more AHA messages, you'll begin to see how these books contextually apply to you. AHAthat/THiNKaha books advocate for continuous, lifelong learning. They will help you transform your AHAs into actionable items with tangible results until you no longer have to say AHA to these moments—they'll become part of your daily practice as you continue to grow and learn.

Mitchell Levy, The AHA Guy at AHAthat
publisher@thinkaha.com

THiNKaha®

Contents

The higher your #SelfLove and #Confidence, the greater success you will achieve. #HighlySuccessfulWomen

Caryn Ross

http://aha.pub/SuccessfulWomen

Share the AHA messages from this book socially by going to
http://aha.pub/SuccessfulWomen

Section I
Why This Book Will Change Your Life

As women, we are known to be great multitaskers, risk takers, and task managers, but do we do this with self-care and compassion for ourselves? Or are we striving to exceed our expectations and grasp that goal of perfection—or at least, near perfection? Does this then lead down a path of self-criticism, questioning, fear of failure, and less love for oneself?

One key ingredient that drives the success of highly successful positive women is the ability to have a focused positive mindset. Highly successful women believe in others and most importantly, in themselves, and project that outwardly. Their focus is not on the "lack of" in their lives, but rather "abundance of." They truly love themselves, are passionate, and work at an energy level that empowers those who surround them. The higher self-love and self-confidence they have, the greater success they achieve. More learning and exploration unfolds, better mood shifts occur and there is a continuous motivation to take initiative and push toward goals and outcomes.

The moment you shift your thoughts and mindset, this will lead to a path of self-love and awareness. I welcome you to begin this journey and take the messages delivered in this book to break old limiting cycles and explore your true inner self. Even trying three messages a day, you will see the transformation happen into the leader you are, with the ability to empower in a positive light. Believe in yourself and you will see remarkable results!

1

#SelfLove is the key to everything, and
the key to loving oneself is to continually
realign your why, be fearless, regulate
the ego, forgive, and change the mindset.
#HighlySuccessfulWomen

_____

_____

_____

2

Love, security, and success come from within.
Look inwardly to achieve what you want in
life. #SelfLove #HighlySuccessfulWomen

_____

_____

_____

3

The higher your #SelfLove and #Confidence, the greater success you will achieve. #HighlySuccessfulWomen

_____

_____

_____

4

Do you do things with self-care and compassion for your self? #HighlySuccessfulWomen do!

_____

_____

_____

5

The most terrifying thing is to accept oneself completely. —C.G. Jung
via Caryn Ross
#HighlySuccessfulWomen

_____

_____

_____

6

"Love yourself first and everything else falls into line. You really have to love yourself to get anything done in this world."
—Lucille Ball via Caryn Ross
#HighlySuccessfulWomen

_____

_____

_____

7

What is the key ingredient that drives the success of #HighlySuccessfulWomen?
A #PositiveMindset!

_____

_____

_____

8

#HighlySuccessfulWomen focus not on the "lack of" in their lives, but rather "abundance of." What are you focusing on? #SelfLove

_____

_____

_____

9

Don't sacrifice your needs over others to obtain your happiness. It is OK to put yourself first and choose your dreams. #SelfLove #HighlySuccessfulWomen

_____

_____

_____

10

When you manifest #SelfLove in your life, you can break your stagnant cycles, explore your true inner self, and unlock your full potential. #HighlySuccessfulWomen

_____

_____

_____

I ♥ ME

When people start seeing you respect yourself, they're going to respect you as well. #SelfLove #HighlySuccessfulWomen

Caryn Ross
http://aha.pub/SuccessfulWomen

Share the AHA messages from this book socially by going to
http://aha.pub/SuccessfulWomen

Section II
It's Really about YOU

The journey of self-love is to be intentional of who you really are, not who you personify. What is your powerbase? First, it starts with care for your health, your soul, and your heart. Nourish yourself with healthy activities for the mind and body. Surround yourself with individuals who support you. Trust your instincts, and focus your intentions on what you want, not what you don't want. One trick to this is to remember that society does not dictate and influence your overall happiness and success—you do.

We sometimes fall into what is called pre-conditions. For example, your family may have been critical growing up, so you criticize yourself. These continual behavioral patterns condition the mind to think in a limiting way, which leads to beating ourselves up. Instead of playing this victim game, start to take care of yourself and recondition your thoughts. Every day, start with personal affirmations and carry them with you. Many are included here, so pick a few, create your own, and read them each day.

Keep an open door to continual learning. Listen to an audiobook, read a book that uplifts you, or take ten minutes during lunch to read an article that will inspire your work. Take an online course to learn a new skill. This trains your mind to adapt and grow, and this self-improvement will lead to your best successes. Remember that there are no closed doors and to continually surround yourself with people and circumstances that promote your growth.

11

What is one thing you love about yourself?
Tell yourself every morning in front of the
mirror. #SelfLove #HighlySuccessfulWomen

_____

_____

_____

12

Successful women goal set and visualize it.
Start a journal. Write three goals and
at least two forward actions to obtain
these goals. #Inspire others.
#HighlySuccessfulWomen

_____

_____

_____

13

Reflect on what you really want, not on
what you want in that specific moment.
#HighlySuccessfulWomen

_____

_____

_____

14

If you separate your personal and professional lives, it will be nearly impossible to create a successful holistic you. #HighlySuccessfulWomen understand this.

_____

_____

_____

15

#HighlySuccessfulWomen are successful because both their personal and professional lives are aligned. Are yours?

_____

_____

_____

16

Be happy around others, and radiate positive vibes in order to put a smile on everyone's face, despite the crazy day ahead. #HighlySuccessfulWomen

_____

_____

_____

17

Don't let your inner critic take you down,
you condition yourself toward negativity
every day without even realizing it.
Stop criticizing yourself! #SelfLove
#HighlySuccessfulWomen

_____

_____

_____

18

If you don't respect other people, they
will not respect you. Do you want to be
respected and loved? Love yourself first.
#HighlySuccessfulWomen

_____

_____

_____

19

When people start seeing you respect yourself, they're going to respect you as well. #SelfLove #HighlySuccessfulWomen

_____

_____

_____

20

Take a step back from everything that's keeping you busy, and do something that will make you feel good. #SelfLove #HighlySuccessfulWomen

_____

_____

_____

21

Make space for yourself today, without filling it with a lot of people and activities. #SelfLove #HighlySuccessfulWomen

_____

_____

_____

22

Connect with nature today. Take a walk, sit out in the sun, and enjoy the warmth. Do yard work or plant something. #SelfLove #HighlySuccessfulWomen

_____

_____

_____

23

Try a new healthier habit, food, exercise routine, and brain exercise. Stimulate yourself in ways you never imagined. #SelfLove #HighlySuccessfulWomen

_____

_____

_____

24

Find a champion who loves and supports you to help you empower yourself and boost your #SelfLove and #SelfConfidence. #HighlySuccessfulWomen

_____

_____

_____

25

#Affirmations are positive statements that guide your subconscious mind to change the way you think. Write down three affirmations that you should say to yourself every day. #HighlySuccessfulWomen

_____

_____

_____

26

Set affirmations each day, journal them, and if one does not happen, celebrate that you still did a great job and realign for the next day. #HighlySuccessfulWomen

_____

_____

_____

27

1 of 5 #SelfLove Mantras: My goals and aspirations are destined for success. It is okay to live the dream. #HighlySuccessfulWomen

_____

_____

_____

28

2 of 5 #SelfLove Mantras: I am strong and decisive, and today, I am going to consciously make at least three concise decisions. #HighlySuccessfulWomen

_____

_____

_____

29

3 of 5 #SelfLove Mantras: My intelligence and beauty are a great combination to manifest anything I wrap my head around. #HighlySuccessfulWomen

_____

_____

_____

30

4 of 5 #SelfLove Mantras: I am a hard worker; I know my limitations and work with them to grow every day. What is the limitation I can improve on today? #HighlySuccessfulWomen

_____

_____

_____

31

5 of 5 #SelfLove Mantras: I said no to others and said yes to myself. The sun still came up the next day. #HighlySuccessfulWomen

_____

_____

_____

32

Start eliminating one obstacle a day that prevents you from achieving your goals and loving yourself. #SelfLove #HighlySuccessfulWomen

_____

_____

_____

33

A leader who has #SelfConfidence and #SelfLove paints positivity and affirmation on everyone they interact with. #HighlySuccessfulWomen

_____

_____

_____

Do small, manageable steps that will ensure that you stay on the right path to accomplish your goals.
#Affirmation #HighlySuccessfulWomen

BE **HERE** **NOW**

Caryn Ross
http://aha.pub/SuccessfulWomen

Share the AHA messages from this book socially by going to
http://aha.pub/SuccessfulWomen

Section III
Continually Realign the WHY

Self-awareness is our ability to control who we are, to understand our strengths and weaknesses with acceptance, and to fully appreciate ourselves to create positive change. Without it, we are incapable of realizing our true self and those of others. Becoming emotionally aware and learning how to manage it through self-regulation will lead to positive outward results. This includes leading by example, the ability to accept feedback to learn and grow, and continually being able to realign the why to harness our passion and accomplish all our goals.

When we invoke our inner why and purpose through self-love, it will enable us to face any challenges and tap into our highest potential. You become powered with a clear purpose and inwardly believe what your greatest value is through employing your strengths and believing in yourself. This is where the greatest successes occur. It is more difficult to wait for perfection rather than just focusing on progression.

34

Seek opportunities that align with your "why" to gain clarity of what you truly want. #HighlySuccessfulWomen

_____

_____

_____

35

If you are not in ACT (Action Changes Thoughts) mode, then you cannot re-align to reach your desired outcomes. #HighlySuccessfulWomen

_____

_____

_____

36

Perfection is not an attainable goal. If you treat it as such, you will continually beat yourself up when you make a mistake. #HighlySuccessfulWomen

_____

_____

_____

37

Discover the reason that fires you up each day, and align yourself around what will support it. #HighlySuccessfulWomen

_____

_____

_____

38

Do small, manageable steps that will ensure that you stay on the right path to accomplish your goals. #Affirmation. #HighlySuccessfulWomen

_____

_____

_____

39

Celebrate your triumph after accomplishing your #Affirmation for the day, then move to your second one. #HighlySuccessfulWomen

_____

_____

_____

40

Don't set impossible goals only to beat yourself up when not met and feed negative thought. #Realign #HighlySuccessfulWomen

_____

_____

_____

41

When negative things do happen, remember that the sun will still shine the next day. #TryAgain #HighlySuccessfulWomen

_____

_____

_____

42

To understand your why, ask yourself what you know already, what you need to learn, if you value it, and if it inspires you to greater things. #HighlySuccessfulWomen

_____

_____

_____

43

Distractions are part of our lives. Continually #Realign your WHY in order to stay on the right path. #HighlySuccessfulWomen

_____

_____

_____

44

Realignment comes with evaluating distractions and re-executing your plans to work on them. #HighlySuccessfulWomen don't allow distractions to stop them.

_____

_____

_____

45

When your personal and professional lives are not aligned, you'll be seen as an inauthentic person. #HighlySuccessfulWomen embody their true self all the time.

_____

_____

_____

46

Learn from feedback from others.
Appreciate it and grow from it. We
all have room to improve and grow.
#HighlySuccessfulWomen

_____

_____

_____

47

Make regular weekly check-ins with
yourself, and review if you are meeting your
personal and professional goals. #Realign
#HighlySuccessfulWomen

_____

_____

_____

48

Don't think that everything's just going to fall into place and that the universe is going to take care of itself, because it's not. #Realign #TakeAction #HighlySuccessfulWomen

_____

_____

_____

49

When opportunities come your way, do you see them as presents or do you ignore them? #Mindset #HighlySuccessfulWomen

_____

_____

_____

50

If you keep asking for opportunities but ignore them, it's the same as not asking for them at all. #Mindset #HighlySuccessfulWomen

_____

_____

_____

51

Society places a negative mindset on ourselves. Be firm in your belief that you will achieve whatever you want to achieve. #Affirmation #HighlySuccessfulWomen

_____

_____

_____

52

Feeling miserable? Think of three things you can do to change tomorrow and make you happier. #HighlySuccessfulWomen

_____

_____

_____

53

Find five minutes each morning where you can relax your mind and #Reaffirm three great things you want to do in your day to be a better person. #HighlySuccessfulWomen

_____

_____

_____

54

When you start doubting your self-worth, process it, accept it, don't dwell, and then #Realign yourself to get back on track. #SelfLove #HighlySuccessfulWomen

_____

_____

_____

55

The only competition you should be in is with yourself. Whom are you competing with? #Realign #HighlySuccessfulWomen

_____

_____

_____

56

Your goals and objectives may change sometimes because something great manifested in your life. Even so, you still need to continually #Realign your WHY. #HighlySuccessfulWomen

_____

_____

_____

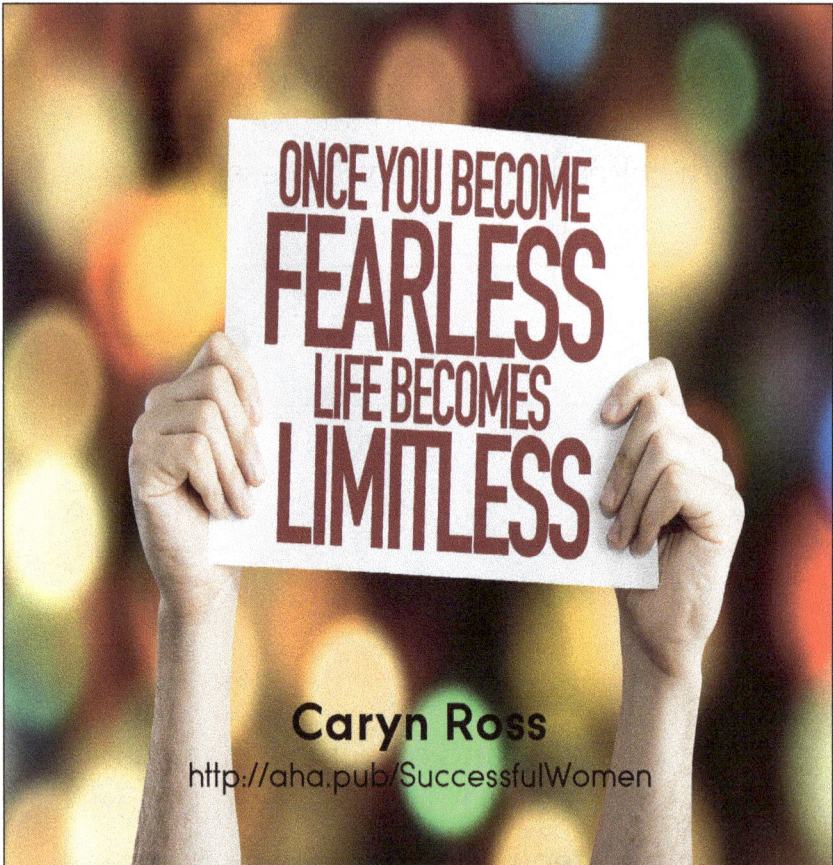

ONCE YOU BECOME
FEARLESS
LIFE BECOMES
LIMITLESS

Caryn Ross
http://aha.pub/SuccessfulWomen

Share the AHA messages from this book socially by going to
http://aha.pub/SuccessfulWomen

Section IV
Be Fearless, Not Fearful

Don't fear—it's that simple. In order for any transformation to happen and manifest your desired outcomes, you need to "unstick" yourself and be fearless doing it. Don't we all have a moment where we feel stuck but have some fear of making a change to unstick? You can't be fearless if you don't accept what you fear, because this often swings us back into our comfort zones, and thus, we don't reach our goals. To grow and change, it takes a level of getting uncomfortable to get comfortable again.

Remember that failure is a great thing! It gives you the ability to learn, grow, and assess what you need to change to get better, rework, or maybe just move away from it. You may even find new opportunities and different paths that lead you to even greater outcomes. Highly successful women embrace failures and are fearless doing it because they recognize that it allows for ideation, innovation, and growth of yourself inwardly.

57

#BeFearless in the pursuit of what sets your soul on fire. —Jennifer Lee via #HighlySuccessfulWomen

_____

_____

_____

58

You have to get uncomfortable to get comfortable. To get really uncomfortable, you have to #BeFearless. #HighlySuccessfulWomen

_____

_____

_____

59

#HighlySuccessfulWomen did something they were uncomfortable with doing, which brought out their greatest successes. #BeFearless

_____

_____

_____

60

#HighlySuccessfulWomen always have a story about how their success was due to not being fearful. #BeFearless

_____

_____

_____

61

People don't like change because change
creates fear. #HighlySuccessfulWomen
change and adapt.

_____

_____

_____

62

Are you in a miserable position? Move! Be #Fearless! #HighlySuccessfulWomen

_____

_____

_____

63

If you like to stay in the safety of your comfort zone, you can't complain when things are not changing for you. #TakeAction #BeFearless #HighlySuccessfulWomen

_____

_____

_____

64

We are only responsible for our own actions. Don't fear the possible outcomes — fear staying stuck. #BeFearless #HighlySuccessfulWomen

_____

_____

_____

65

Fear is a wakeup call, not the time
to go take a nap. #BeFearless
#HighlySuccessfulWomen

_____

_____

_____

66

Remove those fear-based thoughts to change the outcomes of your life. Switch one negative thought into two positive thoughts. #BeFearless #HighlySuccessfulWomen

---

67

Recognize your triumphs over your fears. #Mindset #BeFearless #HighlySuccessfulWomen

68

Reward yourself with something indulgent when you overcome a fear. You deserve it! #BeFearless #HighlySuccessfulWomen

_____

_____

_____

69

Write the one thing that you are most fearful of in your career, and ask yourself why. #BeFearless #HighlySuccessfulWomen

_____

_____

_____

70

List three things you fear the most and three solutions to call action to them. #BeFearless #HighlySuccessfulWomen

_____

_____

_____

71

When in a moment of doubt, go to one thing that you know will pull you from the quicksand and take back your power. #BeFearless #HighlySuccessfulWomen

_____

_____

_____

72

Listen to yourself, your soul, your gut. It will guide you and allow you to take risks without fear. #BeFearless #HighlySuccessfulWomen

_____

_____

_____

73

Nobody can ensure that failure is not going to happen. #HighlySuccessfulWomen are #Fearless no matter what.

_____

_____

_____

74

Everybody has experienced failure.
#HighlySuccessfulWomen don't fear
failure; they embrace it and learn from it.
#BeFearless

_____

_____

_____

75

There is no leader who hasn't failed at one point. They got up, learned from it, and stayed focused and #Fearless. #HighlySuccessfulWomen

_____

_____

_____

76

When negative things do happen, remember that the sun will still shine the next day. #TryAgain #HighlySuccessfulWomen

_____

_____

_____

77

Setbacks are what challenge you,
not what stop you. #BeFearless
#HighlySuccessfulWomen

_____

_____

_____

78

Recondition yourself and learn something new from negative things to manifest them more positively in your life. #HighlySuccessfulWomen

_____

_____

_____

79

If you open your mind to problems and manifest them in a positive manner, you can change it. #Mindset #HighlySuccessfulWomen

_____

_____

_____

80

If you could change one thing in your life, knowing your desired outcome would be reached, what would it be? Have fun but keep it realistic. #HighlySuccessfulWomen

_____

_____

_____

81

Nothing in your life will transform if you're fearful of what's going to happen. #BeFearless #HighlySuccessfulWomen

_____

_____

_____

82

Don't be fearful of the future. When you go back and forth in your decision-making, you lose opportunities. #BeFearless #HighlySuccessfulWomen

_____

_____

_____

83

What's the best and worst thing that could happen if you #MoveForward? #BeFearless #HighlySuccessfulWomen

_____

_____

_____

84

#HighlySuccessfulWomen don't detach
from their instinct and allow others
to drive their fears. #BeFearless

_____

_____

_____

85

Don't let fear limit you from moving
forward and succeeding. #BeFearless
#HighlySuccessfulWomen

_____

_____

_____

86

Be thankful for what you have,
#BeFearless for what you want.
—Joel Osteen via Caryn Ross
#HighlySuccessfulWomen

_____

_____

_____

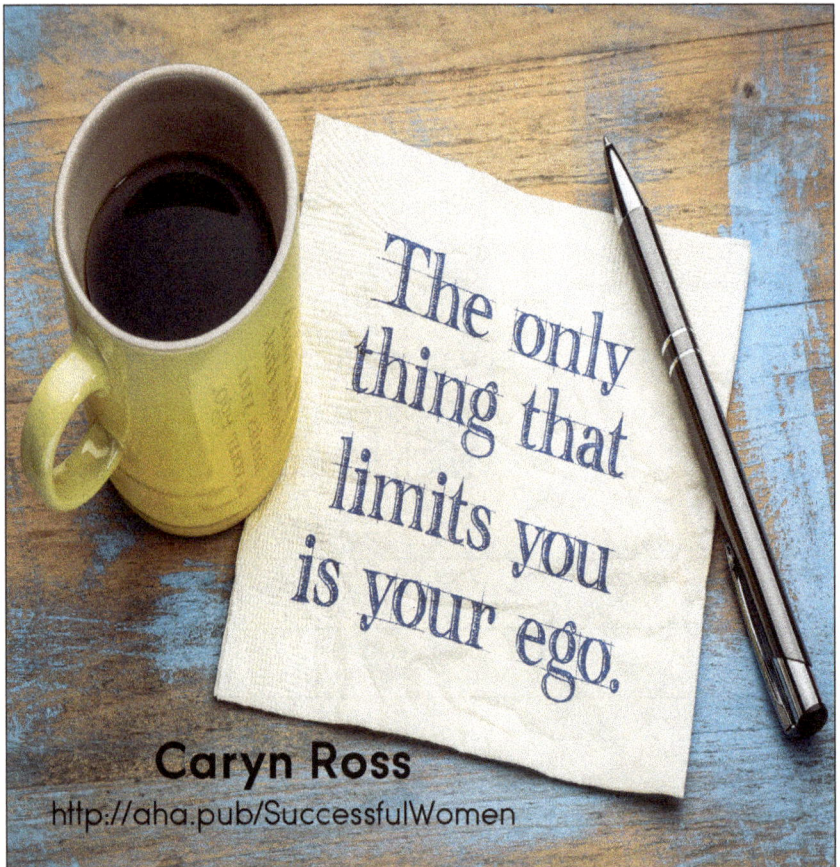

The only
thing that
limits you
is your ego.

Caryn Ross
http://aha.pub/SuccessfulWomen

Share the AHA messages from this book socially by going to
http://aha.pub/SuccessfulWomen

Section V
Keep the Ego in Check

The ego is what creates our emotions, reactions, and pain. Everyone lives in ego, and the ego is bound to take hits when you are rejected or when disappointment occurs. Your ego thinks that everything has to be perfect to be happy, but life circumstances are not always peaches and cream. Then we invite in negativity, which transforms into unproductive thoughts and again, sticks us.

Or the opposite occurs: We allow the ego to shift into high gear, where we get so filled with ego, we begin to think we are the best and no one knows better than us. That's when we stop growing and learning and fall into lower productivity, which results in lower self-esteem and confidence. Growth is about getting over your sense of entitlement that everyone else is wrong. What is more important? To be right or to be happy?

Challenge yourself, and look hard at your ego and how it may stop you from success. For example, if you were passed on a promotion, don't over-analyze it—life is full of experiences that we can continually over-analyze. When we do that, we are not trusting ourselves inwardly, but letting the ego manifest into thoughts that deter us from our path. Instead, get back to your self-love and ask, "What is right for me? What can I do better next time? Where do I need to grow?" Look at your ego as an invitation to reconnect with yourself.

87

Keep the #Ego in check through recognizing that self-love is the GPS to a steady path. #HighlySuccessfulWomen

_____

_____

_____

88

Your #Ego is a reserve and like a gas tank, should be used, replenished, and depleted. #Regulate #HighlySuccessfulWomen

_____

_____

_____

89

Does it take a big #Ego or a powerful self-image to be successful? #Regulate #HighlySuccessfulWomen

_____

_____

_____

90

Pick which driver is behind your decision making — your ego or self-love — to determine your worth. #HighlySuccessfulWomen

_____

_____

_____

91

The battle of #SelfLove vs #Ego, which do you want to win? #HighlySuccessfulWomen

_____

_____

_____

92

If you know that you're capable of succeeding, then how can you stop your negative #Ego from doubting? #DialItUp #HighlySuccessfulWomen

_____

_____

_____

93

Learn from your #Ego, then get away from it to give yourself insightfulness and move forward. #HighlySuccessfulWomen

_____

_____

_____

94

#HighlySuccessfulWomen stop hesitating and use their #Ego to propel themselves and face their fears.

_____

_____

_____

95

If you don't like the way someone is speaking to you, set your #Ego aside and just pay attention to the content instead of the delivery. Listen for the message. #HighlySuccessfulWomen

_____

_____

_____

96

"You never really understand a person until you consider things from his point of view ... until you climb into his skin and walk around in it." —Atticus Finch. Do you walk in the shoes of others? #HighlySuccessfulWomen

_____

_____

_____

97

Stop the blame game when things don't go your way. #Reflect instead of feeding the #Ego. #HighlySuccessfulWomen

_____

_____

_____

98

During a heated discussion, can you just back down and let it go for the greater good? #Ego #HighlySuccessfulWomen

_____

_____

_____

99

Regulate yourself so others won't have to. #Ego #HighlySuccessfulWomen

_____

_____

_____

100

The examples we set are the most powerful teaching tools. Keep your #Ego in check. #HighlySuccessfulWomen

_____

_____

_____

101

Leave your #Ego at the door every morning, and just do some truly great work. Few things will make you feel better than a job brilliantly done. —Robin S. Sharma via Caryn Ross #HighlySuccessfulWomen

_____

_____

102

Leadership is not a popularity contest; it's about leaving your ego at the door. The name of the game is to lead without a title. —Robin S. Sharma via Caryn Ross #HighlySuccessfulWomen

---

103

Utilize your #Ego in low moments as a reminder of the amazing things you are capable of. #HighlySuccessfulWomen

---

104

#HighlySuccessfulWomen feed themselves love without #Ego interference. #SelfLove

_____

_____

_____

105

Don't be your own worst enemy; be your greatest supporter. Regulate your #Ego. #HighlySuccessfulWomen

_____

_____

_____

The moment you recognize that you need #Forgiveness, you're already halfway toward forgiving yourself. #HighlySuccessfulWomen

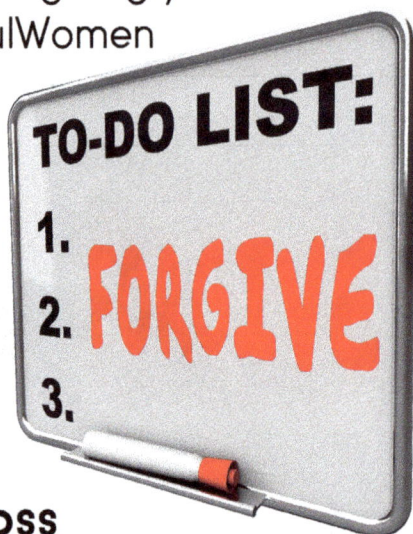

TO-DO LIST:

1.

2. *FORGIVE*

3.

Caryn Ross

http://aha.pub/SuccessfulWomen

Share the AHA messages from this book socially by going to
http://aha.pub/SuccessfulWomen

Section VI
Forgive, Release, and Re-energize

We all beat ourselves up from time to time over past mistakes and regrets, which then allow us to think that we are not good enough. The result is a conditioning of our mind that we are not worthy or deserving, and then we may become resentful and judgmental. It is easier to say, "If it wasn't for this experience, I would be happier."

You can't change the past, but you can change your present thoughts by NOT dwelling or living with regret. Instead, forgive others and yourself, because if you cannot forgive yourself first, then you will continue to manifest those negative thoughts, which in turn, can lead to lower self-worth and fuel anxiety and fear. Stop cultivating your inner bully. Have you ever met a perfect person?

It is all about reprogramming your thoughts. Change the mindset, and say that these past experiences are great learning experiences. Identify and take your life lessons and move forward. Give up the hope that anything could have been different—the "would have," "should have," and "could have." Have self-compassion and be kind to yourself even in your worst moments. You can't change your past, but you can learn and propel the lessons into your future outcomes.

106

Never underestimate yourself because of past actions. Instead, #Forgive and set your mindset that you can accomplish anything. #HighlySuccessfulWomen

_____

_____

_____

107

The moment you recognize that you need #Forgiveness, you're already halfway toward forgiving yourself. #HighlySuccessfulWomen

_____

_____

_____

108

When you have hurt someone, authentically ask for forgiveness, then #Forgive yourself, whether they accept your apology or not. #HighlySuccessfulWomen

_____

_____

_____

109

When you forgive at work, the best outcomes can manifest, including a more productive, harmonious environment. #HighlySuccessfulWomen

_____

_____

_____

110

Don't justify your wrongdoings. Just apologize for it, and state how you are going to change so it doesn't happen again. #MoveForward #HighlySuccessfulWomen

_____

_____

_____

111

When you make mistakes, #Forgive
yourself and learn from it so it
doesn't manifest again in the future.
#HighlySuccessfulWomen

_____

_____

_____

112

Stop the blame game; we are only accountable for our own actions. #Forgive #HighlySuccessfulWomen

_____

_____

_____

113

Don't allow others to invade your thoughts; the best revenge is just to #Forgive and let it go. #MoveForward #HighlySuccessfulWomen

_____

_____

_____

114

#Release your anger, disappointment, and hurt. Don't let it fester, because things will just get worse. #Forgive #HighlySuccessfulWomen

_____

_____

_____

115

Let resentment go; the more you hold onto it, the more anger will fester. #Forgive #MoveForward #HighlySuccessfulWomen

_____

_____

_____

116

Don't dwell if you missed the deadline; take the repercussion and change your habit so it doesn't happen again. #MoveForward #HighlySuccessfulWomen

_____

_____

_____

117

When you learn from your mistakes and change, you get the forgiveness you need to #MoveForward and #ReEnergize. #HighlySuccessfulWomen

_____

_____

_____

118

Get over the guilt, change something to ensure it never happens again, and make somebody's life a bit better. #ReEnergize #HighlySuccessfulWomen

_____

_____

_____

119

If you're feeling guilty, give yourself permission to do something good for the world. #ReEnergize #HighlySuccessfulWomen

_____

_____

_____

120

The way you speak to yourself in your mind will translate the same to the outside world. What are you saying to yourself? #HighlySuccessfulWomen

_____

_____

_____

121

Don't let self-criticism manifest; it is okay to #Forgive, be forgiven, and #MoveForward. #HighlySuccessfulWomen

_____

_____

_____

122

Process emotions; feel what you want to feel, learn from it, improve it, and #MoveForward. Do you process your emotions positively? You should! #HighlySuccessfulWomen

_____

_____

_____

123

Reflect on two past mistakes, and list two things you learned from them. What have you changed moving forward? #HighlySuccessfulWomen

_____

_____

_____

124

Ask yourself: What two life lessons gave you opportunities to #Learn and #Grow? #HighlySuccessfulWomen

_____

_____

_____

125

Have gratitude for what you learned from your experiences and how they placed you back in check. #BeGrateful #HighlySuccessfulWomen

_____

_____

_____

126

You can't change the past or the outcomes of the past. All you can do is #Forgive others, yourself, and #MoveForward. #HighlySuccessfulWomen

_____

_____

_____

127

Remind yourself that when mistakes occur, you are not the mistake. #Forgive, #Release, and #ReEnergize. #HighlySuccessfulWomen

_____

_____

_____

128

Say no to dwelling on the past, as it can manifest into an addiction. #SayYes to your future. #HighlySuccessfulWomen

_____

_____

_____

129

Who wins if you #Forgive? YOU! #MoveForward #HighlySuccessfulWomen

_____

_____

_____

BELIEVE IN YOURSELF

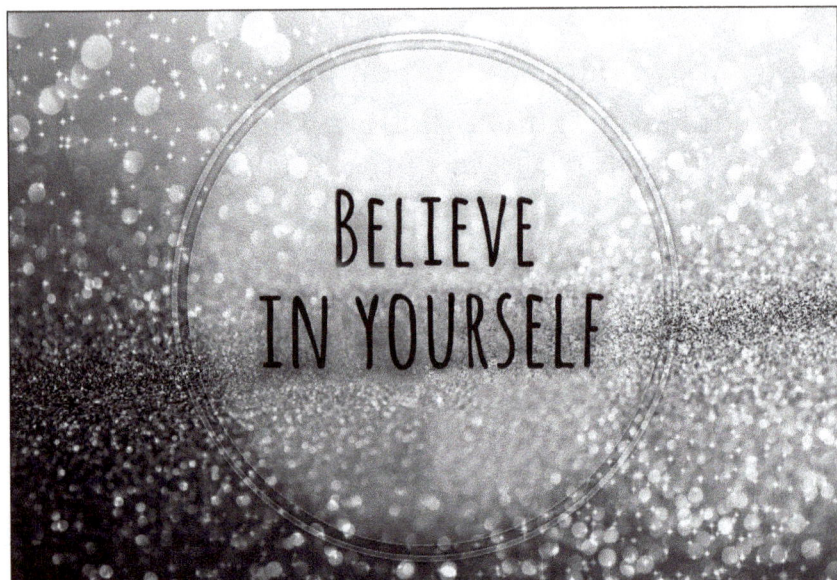

It's alright to realize that you're not perfect, and it's alright to make a mistake. #SelfLove #HighlySuccessfulWomen

Caryn Ross

http://aha.pub/SuccessfulWomen

Share the AHA messages from this book socially by going to
http://aha.pub/SuccessfulWomen

Section VII
Self-Love Is the Key to Success

Today starts with you! When you change your mindset and walk on the path of self-love and awareness, nothing will hold you back. Every day, give yourself doses of self-love. Yes, there may be days that you will be exhausted doing this, feeling like it isn't manifesting. But to unstick, you need discomfort to evolve the change and roll through the transition. Start by incorporating three to five of these messages in your daily routine, and the results will follow. You have all the power to control the circumstances in your life through your thoughts and inward love of yourself. Continuously push and challenge yourself. Believe that you are the valuable important woman you are, and you will see all the amazing changes that come your way.

When you start loving yourself, you can break the stagnant cycles happening in your life and explore your true inner self. Surround yourself with those who support your journey and bring out your best qualities. Remember to take care of your inner and outer self to be the best version of yourself. Always take the time to respect yourself. Empower others and have compassion doing it. Lastly, know that your core foundation starts with self-love to be that successful woman you are destined to be.

130

#SelfLove creates the ability to stay on track and in balance, which results in a clear vision of success. #HighlySuccessfulWomen

_____

_____

_____

131

You are capable of loving yourself. Treasure your value and don't lose sight of it. #SelfLove #HighlySuccessfulWomen

_____

_____

_____

132

Do you love your job? Or do you love being a change-maker at your job and making a difference in people's lives? #HighlySuccessfulWomen

_____

_____

_____

133

Stop saying that you're not worthy. Start saying, "I deserve good things and I'm worthy of happiness." #SelfLove #HighlySuccessfulWomen

_____

_____

_____

134

Negative things are not going to happen unless you allow it. #SelfLove #HighlySuccessfulWomen

_____

_____

_____

135

Even if you're in a bad situation right now, that doesn't mean it will always be that way. #ChangeYourMindset #BePositive #HighlySuccessfulWomen

_____

_____

_____

136

#HighlySuccessfulWomen know how to switch their mindset to get back on track with #SelfLove so negativity doesn't catch them.

_____

_____

_____

137

Don't let the preconditioned notion of what you grew up with define you and what you need to do. #SelfLove #HighlySuccessfulWomen

_____

_____

_____

138

It's alright to realize that you're not perfect, and it's alright to make a mistake. #SelfLove #HighlySuccessfulWomen

_____

_____

_____

139

How to achieve your goals?
#ChangeYourMindset, believe in it, and
keep to it. #HighlySuccessfulWomen

_____

_____

_____

140

Life is not going to be perfect. What are you going to do tomorrow to get yourself back on track and remind yourself of who you are? #SelfLove #HighlySuccessfulWomen

_____

_____

_____

About the Author

Caryn Ross, The Aha Ignitor, is a mindset business coach, speaker, trainer, and founder of SpectaBridge Solutions (https://SpectaBridgeSolutions.com), which helps executives, entrepreneurs, innovators, and business owners lead and transform their organizations and businesses to explosive levels of productivity and profitability.

Early in her career while interfacing with C-Suite executives, Caryn developed a keen appreciation for how collaboration and relationships interact with communications and self-confidence, driving successful business results. She looks to ignite a culture of confidence and transformational leadership to help businesses and individuals get "unstuck" and uncover their own unique AHA moments.

Through individual coaching, speaking, webinars, and workshops, Caryn creates unique value-add tools and strategies. These are designed to consistently inspire others to take action, enable impactful connections, create dynamic employees, improve client experiences, and empower leadership with a business mindset. Her goal is to propel others to grow and be highly successful achieving all their desired goals.

AHAthat®

THiNKaha has created AHAthat for you to share content from this book.

- ➲ Share each AHA message socially:
  http://aha.pub/SuccessfulWomen
- ➲ Share additional content: https://AHAthat.com
- ➲ Info on authoring: https://AHAthat.com/Author

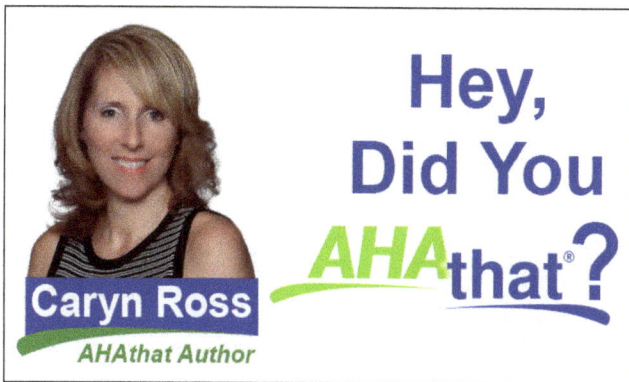

Hey, Did You AHAthat®?

Caryn Ross
AHAthat Author

www.ingramcontent.com/pod-product-compliance
Lightning Source LLC
Chambersburg PA
CBHW071208200326
41519CB00018B/5424